Wolfgang Amadeus Mozart
Musical Genius

Stewart Ross

HODDER
Wayland

an imprint of Hodder Children's Books

© 2003 White-Thomson Publishing Ltd

Produced by White-Thomson Publishing Ltd
2/3 St Andrew's Place, Lewes, BN7 1UP

Editor: Elaine Fuoco-Lang
Inside and cover design: Tim Mayer
Picture Research: Shelley Noronha –
    Glass Onion Pictures
Proofreader: Alison Cooper

Cover: A portrait of Mozart as a young boy.
Title page: Wolfgang Amadeus Mozart, the Austrian
composer in later life.

Published in Great Britain in 2003 by Hodder Wayland,
an imprint of Hodder Children's Books.

British Library Cataloguing in Publication Data
Ross, Stewart
    Wolfgang Amadeus Mozart. - (Famous Lives)
    1. Mozart, Wolfgang Amadeus, 1756-1791 - Juvenile
    literature 2. Composers - Austria - Biography - Juvenile
    literature I. Title
    780.9'2

ISBN 0 7502 4321 X

Printed in Hong Kong

Hodder Children's Books
An division of Hodder Headline Limited
338 Euston Road, London, NW1 3BH

Picture acknowledgements
The publisher would like to thank the following for their
kind permission to use these pictures:
AKG cover, 5, 6, 7, 8, 9, 11, 12-13, 14, 15, 17, 18, 19,
21, 23, 24, 25, 26, 27, 28, 29, 30, 31, 32, 33, 34, 35, 36,
39, 40, 41, 43, 44; Bridgeman Art Library 10, 16, 42;
Hodder Wayland Picture Library 22; Mary Evans Picture
Library title page, 4, 20, 37; Redferns 45; Sylvia Corday 38.

CLASS NO.

Contents

The Prodigy

The room was very large and very splendid. The lords and
ladies, courtiers and officials seated within it were among the
grandest of Vienna, the capital city of the mighty Austrian
Empire. The flickering light of hundreds of candles
glimmered and gleamed on their priceless jewels.

Yet the attention of everyone within that room, from the
Count and Countess in the front row to the motionless
footman by the door, was fixed upon a small boy.

*The focus of a young
musician's dreams: the
palace of the Emperor
of Austria in Vienna.*

'... the little child from Salzburg and his sister played the harpsichord. The poor little fellow plays marvellously, he is a Child of the Spirit, lively, charming ...'
Count Karl Zinzendorf, a nobleman from Vienna, writing about Mozart in his diary in 1762.

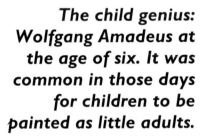

The child genius: Wolfgang Amadeus at the age of six. It was common in those days for children to be painted as little adults.

The six-year-old child sat before a harpsichord. Like his audience, he wore rich clothes of high fashion. At a nod from his father, the boy raised his little hands and began to play. His tiny fingers danced nimbly over the ivory keys, filling the room with music as sweet as summer honey.

The audience smiled and nodded to each other. Yes, this boy from Salzburg was indeed remarkable: Wolfgang Amadeus Mozart was a true prodigy.

Surrounded by Music

Wolfgang Amadeus Mozart was born in the Austrian city of Salzburg on 27 January 1756. Wolfgang Amadeus' father, Leopold Mozart, was a musician. In 1747 he had married Maria Anna Pertl, a young woman from a respectable middle-class family like his own. They had seven children. Only two – Wolfgang Amadeus and his elder sister, who was named Maria Anna after her mother, but known as 'Nannerl' – survived infancy.

'Moreover, I must inform [you] that on 27 January, at 8 p.m., my dear wife was happily delivered of a boy ... now (God be praised) both child and mother are well.'
Leopold Mozart, Mozart's father, writing to a friend on 9 February 1756, about the birth of Mozart.

The house in Salzburg in which Wolfgang Amadeus was born on 27 January 1756. Today it is a museum.

A portrait of Maria Anna, Mozart's mother.

We know little about Wolfgang Amadeus' mother, Maria Anna. A kindly woman, she seems to have left her children's upbringing almost entirely in her husband's hands.

Like most Salzburg musicians, Leopold was employed by the prince-archbishop. In 1757 he was promoted to court composer. He was a talented violinist and a successful music teacher. His handbook on violin teaching (1756) was translated into several languages. From the moment of his birth, therefore, the young Wolfgang Amadeus was surrounded by music.

'A Miracle'

By Wolfgang Amadeus' third birthday, Leopold and Maria Anna realized he was no normal child. He had enormous energy, both mental and physical, and staggering talents. At four he could draw, solve mathematical problems and use words expertly.

Above all, he had an amazing musical instinct. He seemed to discover music within him rather than learn it. It was as if he had been born with a musical soul.

Wolfgang Amadeus playing the violin with his sister and father.

King Joseph introduces the young Wolfgang Amadeus to his mother, the Empress Maria Theresa, October 1762. Painted more than 100 years later (1869), the picture is a romantic recreation of the scene.

By five Wolfgang Amadeus was composing simple pieces. He had learned to play the clavier (an early form of piano) and violin well – but he hated the trumpet. Its harsh sound offended his sensitive ears.

Leopold could hardly believe his son's abilities. A man of strong religious faith, he decided such talent must be a gift from God. It was his duty, therefore, to nurture the gift. Leopold also realized that his son's talent would be a welcome source of extra income.

9

Sensible Advice?

In Wolfgang Amadeus' time Western music was totally different from today. Because electricity had not been discovered, music could not be recorded – it was only played and heard live. Sound could not be amplified with microphones and speakers. Nor were there electronic instruments, such as electric guitars.

Many wealthy Italian families held private concert parties where they could experience live music in their own homes.

Joseph 'Papa' Haydn (1732-1809), the son of a wheelwright and the finest composer in Austria before Wolfgang Amadeus. The young Wolfgang dedicated several pieces to Haydn.

'This piece was learned by Wolfgang on 24 January 1761, 3 days before his 5th birthday, between 9 and 9.30 in the evening.' Leopold Mozart, Mozart's father, proudly writing in his daughter Nannerl's music book, in 1761.

The law was also very different from today as it did not protect composers. Anyone could give a public performance of a piece of music or sing a song without paying the composer anything. The composer made money only when someone paid them to write a new piece.

Leopold Mozart knew all these difficulties only too well. From an early age he urged his brilliant son to keep in with the rich – the prince-archbishop of Salzburg, for example. However, even when he was young, Wolfgang Amadeus found his father's sensible advice hard to follow. He knew he was a genius and he was unwilling to grovel to anyone, however rich.

11

On the Road

In 1762 Leopold decided to present his son to the world. He travelled to the German city of Munich with Nannerl and Wolfgang Amadeus. (Germany at that time was several cities and states, not a single country.) Here the children played before the Elector (Prince) of Bavaria.

From Munich the trio moved to Vienna, where we first met Wolfgang Amadeus. Although Nannerl, now aged eleven, was a fine musician, it was the six-year-old Wolfgang Amadeus who stole people's attention. His extraordinary talent even impressed Maria Theresa, the Empress of Austria.

'Master Mozart ... is but Seven Years of Age, plays anything at first sight, and composes amazingly well. He has had the honour of exhibiting before their Majesties greatly to their satisfaction.'
A comment about Mozart's talents in the *Public Advertiser* newspaper, London, 9 May 1764.

The city of Munich, the capital of Bavaria, where Wolfgang and his sister played before the local prince in 1762.

The travel, concerts, music lessons and presentations lasted almost four years. The family visited other parts of Germany, the Low Countries, France and England, where Wolfgang played before King George III (1764).

From every audience the reaction was the same: Wolfgang Amadeus was the most talented young musician anyone had ever heard.

George III, King of Great Britain, 1760-1820, was one of the many grand figures who marvelled at the talents of the young Wolfgang Amadeus.

Father and Son

Wolfgang Amadeus' three-and-a-half-year tour of Europe was an unusual education by our standards. It was not necessarily a poor one, though. The boy met all kinds of people, especially musicians, saw famous sites and learned foreign languages.

The dutiful, organized Leopold kept up his son's musical education, too. The relationship between father and son has always fascinated scholars. Some blame Leopold for being too harsh on the boy, forcing him to grow up too fast and to be so disciplined about his talent.

Entertaining the French nobility: Wolfgang Amadeus, seated at the piano, in Paris in 1763.

A young man at the piano, about 1765: the picture is believed to be of the nine-year-old Wolfgang Amadeus.

Others say that someone as high-spirited as Wolfgang Amadeus needed a steady hand like Leopold's to guide him. Without his father's direction, discipline and pressure, they say, the world might never have seen the genius of Wolfgang Amadeus Mozart.

1767 was spent mainly in Salzburg. Wolfgang Amadeus and Nannerl both caught the deadly smallpox. Happily, they recovered and the next year the twelve-year-old Wolfgang Amadeus was off on his travels again.

Italy and the Opera

Rome as it was at the time of Wolfgang Amadeus.

Wolfgang Amadeus spent much of his teenage years in Italy, a land that adored him. At the time Italy, like Germany, was divided into many cities and states. One of the most powerful of these was Rome, ruled by the pope. Understandably, it was an important centre of religious music. Italy as a whole, however, was most famous for its opera.

16

MITRIDATE

RE DI PONTO.

DRAMMA PER MUSICA
DA RAPPRESENTARSI
NEL REGIO-DUCAL TEATRO
DI MILANO
Nel Carnovale dell' Anno 1771.
DEDICATO
A SUA ALTEZZA SERENISSIMA
IL
DUCA DI MODENA,
REGGIO, MIRANDOLA ec. ec.
AMMINISTRATORE,
E CAPITANO GENERALE
DELLA LOMBARDIA AUSTRIACA
ec. ec.

IN MILANO.)(MDCCLXX.

Nella Stamperia di Giovanni Montani.
M.169a CON LICENZA DE' SUPERIORI.

PERSONAGGI.

MITRIDATE, Re di Ponto, e d'altri Regni, amante d'Aspasia.
Sig. Cavaliere Guglielmo D'Ettore Virtuoso di Camera di S. A. S. Elettorale di Baviera.
ASPASIA, promessa sposa di Mitridate, e già dichiarata Regina,
Signora Antonia Bernasconi.
SIFARE, figliuolo di Mitridate, e di Stratonica, amante d'Aspasia,
Sig. Pietro Benedetti, detto Sartorino.
FARNACE, primo figliuolo di Mitridate, amante della medesima,
Sig. Giuseppe Cicognani.
ISMENE, figlia del Re de' Parti, amante di Farnace,
Signora Anna Francesca Varese.
MARZIO, Tribuno Romano, amico di Farnace,
Sig. Gaspare Bassano.
ARBATE, Governatore di Ninfea,
Sig. Pietro Muschietti.

Compositore della Musica.

Il Sig. Cavaliere Amadeo Wolfgango Mozart, Accademico Filarmonico di Bologna, e Maestro della Musica di Camera di S. A. Rma il Principe, ed Arcivescovo di Salisburgo.

ATTO

M.169b

A programme of one of the first productions of Wolfgang Amadeus' opera Mitridate.

Amazingly, still in his early teens, Wolfgang Amadeus was already writing operas of his own. One, *Mitridate*, was given twenty-one performances in Milan in 1770-1. In the same year he performed another extraordinary feat. He heard the pope's Sistine Choir sing a work – *Miserere* by Gregorio Allegri – known only to themselves. After listening to the piece, Wolfgang wrote out the whole piece from memory!

As a young child Wolfgang Amadeus had been famous as a performer. He still played, of course, but his chief interest was now in composing new music.

The Concert-Master

Mozart's master: Hieronymus Colloredo, the awkward prince-archbishop of Salzburg.

In 1773, aged seventeen, Wolfgang Amadeus asked to work as a musician at the court of Empress Maria Theresa in Vienna. He was rejected. If he had been more humble, he might have succeeded. But Wolfgang Amadeus was not humble and he would not flatter.

Small, bright-eyed and energetic, he said what he thought. He was not arrogant (although he could appear so) but supremely confident in his own talent.

He knew he had a unique ability. More importantly, he wanted to be recognized and to live in the sort of style his talent deserved.

Wolfgang Amadeus felt cramped in Salzburg, particularly after the rather narrow-minded Hieronymus Colloredo became prince-archbishop in 1772. After working as his *Konzertmeister* (concert-master), in 1777 Wolfgang Amadeus set out with his mother for Paris. There, he was sure, his talent would be fully recognized.

Even before he reached Paris, his plans were upset by something unexpected. While travelling through Mannheim, he fell in love.

The River Seine and the Notre Dame Cathedral in Paris. In 1777 Wolfgang Amadeus set out to make his fortune in the city.

Love and Sadness

Wolfgang Amadeus had fallen for Aloysia Weber, the pretty sixteen-year-old daughter of a musician. His mother did not mind the relationship, but his father was furious when he heard of it. His son must concentrate on music alone, he said, and ordered Wolfgang Amadeus to proceed to Paris. The dutiful son, now aged twenty-one, did as he was told.

'I, who from my youth have never been accustomed to look after my own things, linen, clothes and so forth, cannot think of anything I need more than a wife.' Mozart writing to his father saying how he needs a wife.

First love: Wolfgang Amadeus at the piano accompanying Aloysia Weber.

The beginning of the modern orchestral sound: a symphony orchestra at the time of Wolfgang Amadeus.

In Paris the young genius attracted much attention. He earned commissions for new music, including a sparkling concerto for harp and flute. But he was given no well-paid job. More tragically, his mother fell ill and died on 3 July 1778.

Now travelling alone, Wolfgang returned slowly home. His father had arranged for him to be promoted to Colloredo's court organist. Before reaching Salzburg in January 1780, Wolfgang Amadeus called in on the Weber family. Aloysia, now a successful singer, was not interested in him.

21

'The Kindest Heart in the World'

Wolfgang Amadeus was now recognized as the ablest young musician in Germany. It was no surprise when in 1780 the Prince of Munich commissioned him to write a new opera. Called *Idomeneo*, it was warmly praised when first performed early the next year.

The sublime hand: a manuscript of one of Wolfgang Amadeus' early works.

A miniature painting of Constanze Weber at the time of her engagement to Wolfgang Amadeus in 1781.

Fresh from his Munich triumph, Wolfgang Amadeus went to Vienna where prince-archbishop Colloredo was attending the coronation of the new Austrian Emperor, Joseph II. Annoyed at the way the prince-archbishop treated him, Wolfgang Amadeus resigned from his service on 9 June 1781. He was now a free man.

Staying in Vienna with his old friends the Webers, who now lived there, Wolfgang Amadeus fell in love again. His new love was Constanze, Aloysia's eighteen-year-old sister. The couple became engaged at the end of 1781 and were married on 4 August 1782. Although Leopold was not amused, he could do nothing about it. Wolfgang Amadeus had declared his independence.

Unique Talent

With Wolfgang Amadeus at the peak of his creativity, let us take a closer look at his music. Unlike today, there were no obvious barriers between serious (or 'classical') and popular music. Wolfgang Amadeus wrote dances as happily as operas.

All music used similar instruments: strings, woodwind, brass, percussion and keyboards.

Wolfgang Amadeus composed a wide range of pieces. His work ranged from writing for one single instrument to small groups of musicians to large orchestral pieces which would use many different instruments.

The apartment that Wolfgang Amadeus lived in from 1784 to 1787, showing musical instruments from the time.

Johann Sebastian Bach (1685-1750) the composer from north Germany whose music had a profound influence on Wolfgang Amadeus.

Wolfgang Amadeus developed his unique music from what he heard. In London he came across the work of Johann Christian Bach, son of Johann Sebastian Bach who had been the finest musician of a previous generation. In Italy he picked up the native opera style, in Paris the French style of writing for an orchestra. In Vienna he learned from Joseph Haydn, the most respected composer of his day.

Wolfgang Amadeus' brilliant mind absorbed these influences and mixed them with his own genius to produce some of the most remarkable music ever written.

Family Life

After Wolfgang Amadeus' death, Constanze admitted that he had sometimes flirted with servant girls. Nevertheless, their marriage was a very happy one. Her love for him did not fade and she supported him in all he did. For his part, he went to great lengths to keep his 'Stanzerl' (his nickname for Constanze) as happy as possible.

Constanze Mozart in 1782. Wolfgang Amadeus loved her dearly.

Branches of the famous tree: on the left is Franz Xaver Mozart and on the right Karl Thomas Mozart.

'Dearest, most beloved friend ... Everything depends, my only friend, upon whether you can and will lend me another 500 gulden [about £1600].'
Mozart writes a letter begging for money to a friend in 1789.

Between June 1783 and July 1791 the couple had six children. Not unusually for those days, only two – Karl Thomas (born 1784) and Franz Xaver (born 1791) – survived more than six months. Continual childbearing undermined Constanze's health. By the 1790s her medical cures were very expensive.

Husband and wife shared a liking for the high life – fine clothes, servants, a carriage and so forth. Although Wolfgang Amadeus earned far more than most other musicians, he also spent more. The result? Constanze and he were never poor but they were often short of money.

'The Land of the Piano'

Wolfgang Amadeus was the most versatile of composers. The variety of his work was simply staggering. He excelled in all three branches of serious music: chamber music (for a small number of instruments), orchestral music (for the many instruments of an orchestra) and vocal music (for voices).

These musicians are preparing to play as part of an orchestra. Their beautiful clothes suggest they may have played at a special event like a royal banquet.

The romantic young man – a painting of Wolfgang Amadeus produced many years after his death.

Vienna – popularly known as 'the land of the piano' – loved Wolfgang Amadeus and in the year following his marriage his concerts were packed. He composed several sparkling piano concertos (for piano accompanied by an orchestra), grand symphonies and delightful string quartets (for two violins, viola and cello) that built upon Haydn's work. His opera, *Die Entführung* (*The Escape from the Seraglio*), was well received and his religious music reached new depth and maturity with the Coronation Mass.

His only disappointment was the failure to get a job at the court of Emperor Joseph II. This was partly because he was not friendly with the court musicians led by Antonio Salieri.

'It is hardly possible for anyone to stand beside the great Mozart ... It enrages me to think that the unique Mozart has not yet been engaged by an imperial or royal court.'
Joseph Haydn cannot understand why Wolfgang Amadeus does not play at an imperial or royal court.

29

'The Greatest'

In 1785 Wolfgang Amadeus met the librettist (writer) Lorenzo da Ponte. Their partnership produced the glorious opera *The Marriage of Figaro*. It was first staged in Vienna in 1786 and then in Prague.

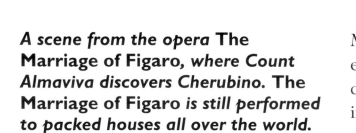

A scene from the opera The Marriage of Figaro, where Count Almaviva discovers Cherubino. The Marriage of Figaro is still performed to packed houses all over the world.

Meanwhile, Joseph Haydn had written to the elderly Leopold Mozart, 'Your son is the greatest composer known to me in person.' This was praise indeed. Others were even more enthusiastic: some said he was the greatest composer ever.

Wolfgang Amadeus recognized his importance and started to make a catalogue of his music. He was also admitted to the Vienna branch of the Freemasons, an exclusive Christian society.

The 29-year-old composer's tragedy was that he had to work unbelievably hard to earn what he felt he deserved. Most other musicians would have been thrilled to have created just one of these works. Wolfgang Amadeus drove himself, month after month, to produce a stream of outstanding compositions. Sadly, as a result of this hard work his health began to suffer.

Another romantic painting of Wolfgang Amadeus – entitled **Mozart Composing***, it tries to capture the ease with which brilliant music came to him.*

Court at Last

Leopold died on 28 May 1787. Although father and son had been living far apart for years, Wolfgang Amadeus was surprised and saddened at the news of his father's death. The man who had created him as a person and a musician was now gone.

There were other family griefs, too. The previous year Constanze's third son had died almost immediately after his birth. In 1787 she gave birth to a daughter who died six months later.

Musically, Wolfgang Amadeus continued to excel. His new opera with da Ponte, *Don Giovanni*, triumphed in Prague.

The eighteenth-century theatre in Prague. The city commissioned Wolfgang Amadeus' opera Don Giovanni and gave its name to his fine Prague Symphony of 1786.

Ludwig van Beethoven, the anxious young composer who impressed Wolfgang Amadeus when they met in 1787.

'Mozart ... went silently to some friends ... and said vivaciously, "Keep your eyes on him; some day he will give the world something to talk about."'
Beethoven, aged 17, recalls meeting Mozart.

Furthermore, the Emperor Joseph II finally gave him a court position, although a minor one. As composer of music for court balls, he produced one of the most famous pieces of chamber music of all time: *Eine kleine Nachtmusik* (*A Little Night Music*).

'Black Thoughts'

By 1788 Wolfgang Amadeus was not as fashionable in Vienna as he had been. Amazingly — in our eyes — the brilliant *Don Giovanni* was not a success when produced in the city. Undaunted, the composer worked on what proved to be his last and greatest symphonies, numbers 39, 40 and 41.

Once, the Emperor Joseph II, an accomplished musician, agreed to sit down and play one of Wolfgang Amadeus' pieces with him. When they were ready, the emperor was surprised to see that the composer had no music before him. Asked where it was, he pointed to his head. 'In there!' he replied with a grin.

'Mozardt's [sic] music is certainly too difficult for the singers.' Emperor Joseph II commenting on the opera *Don Giovanni*.

Pictures from an early production of **Don Giovanni:** *the Don is on the right and one of the women he pursues, Donna Elvira, on the left.*

Joseph II, the emperor of Austria who failed to find an important court position for Wolfgang Amadeus.

Delightful music was not the only thing whirling round Wolfgang Amadeus' mind. He was tired and depressed by his constant lack of money, by the deaths of his children and by Constanze's poor health.

To his dismay, he found 'black thoughts' seeping into his fevered brain.

Debt

Early in 1789 Wolfgang Amadeus was cheered by an invitation to visit the court of the King of Prussia, Frederick William II, one of Germany's most powerful rulers. He travelled to Berlin with Count Karl Lichnowsky via Prague, Dresden and Leipzig. In Berlin he composed chamber pieces with parts specially written for members of the Prussian royal family.

Count Karl Lichnowsky, the wealthy nobleman who helped both Wolfgang Amadeus and, later, Ludwig van Beethoven.

Wolfgang Amadeus towards the end of his life. In reality he would probably have been much leaner than this.

Back in Vienna, his gloom deepened. Constanze gave birth to another daughter, who died almost immediately. The poor mother's medical bills mounted.

The small salary (800 gulden, approximately £2,500) from the Austrian court was not enough to sustain the Mozart household in their accustomed style. To meet the shortfall, Wolfgang Amadeus borrowed heavily, particularly from his Freemason friend, Thomas Puchberg.

'Within 4 months I, the undersigned, shall pay the sum of 100 fl., in words One Hundred Gulden, to Herr von Hofdemel...'
Mozart promises to return the money he borrows from a fellow Freemason for a trip to Berlin.

In the autumn, as Europe reeled with news of a revolution in France, Wolfgang began his third opera with da Ponte. As with his previous works with the same librettist, the commission came from the city of Prague.

37

A Grim Year

The year 1790 was not a good one for the Mozart household. To begin with, Constanze and Wolfgang Amadeus were in poor health. She was exhausted by constant child bearing, he was depressed and plagued by headaches and pains in his joints. Their financial problems did not get any better, either.

The new opera, *Cosi Fan Tutte*, had only five performances. The show was forced to shut down when Joseph II died and the government closed all theatres as a mark of respect.

The health spa at Baden today. In the late eighteenth century Constanze Mozart would have spent many weeks trying to regain her strength at a similar spa in Baden.

38

'Merry dreams!
Quiet, refreshing,
sweet dreams!
Those are the thing!
Dreams which, if
they were realities,
would make
tolerable my life
which has more
of sadness in it
than merriment.'
Mozart writing about
dreams in a letter to
his father, in 1778.
Unfortunately for
Mozart his life
continued to have
more sadness than
happiness in it.

Wolfgang Amadeus wasn't daunted however and saw the coronation of a new emperor as a fresh opportunity for him. He travelled via various wealthy cities in the hope that works might be commissioned from him. He went to the coronation of Leopold II in Frankfurt in 1790 and put on a concert to attract attention.

However, the wretched composer had not chosen his moment well. The concert was poorly attended, he lost money and brought himself nothing but more headaches.

A drawing of the costume design for a production of Wolfgang Amadeus' Cosi Fan Tutte. When this opera was first performed it closed after only a handful of performances.

The Magic Flute

At the turn of the year, things began to improve for the Mozarts. Wolfgang Amadeus was appointed assistant to the elderly *Kapellmeister* (Chapel Master) of St Stephen's Cathedral in Vienna. There was a good chance that he would shortly inherit the well-paid post.

*A drawing of the original production of Wolfgang Amadeus' last and most widely appreciated opera, **The Magic Flute**.*

In the spring an old friend, Emanuel Schikaneder, paid the composer handsomely to write the music for his new opera, *The Magic Flute*. Before it opened, the city of Prague commissioned yet another opera – *La Clemenza di Tito* (*The Clemency of Tito*) – to celebrate the coronation there of Leopold II.

There were other commissions, too, including one for a clarinet concerto. Furthermore, to the delight of both parents, their sixth child, Franz Xaver, was born strong and healthy.

> **'Did I not tell you that I was composing this 'Requiem' for myself?'** Mozart speaking about composing the Requiem as he lay dying.

The strain of all this work told on the composer's health. Moreover, he had also received a strange and somewhat sinister commission: an anonymous figure was paying him to write a requiem. Wolfgang Amadeus had uneasy feelings about who it was for.

Classical glory: a design for a 1799 production of Wolfgang Amadeus' opera **The Clemency of Tito.**

Requiem

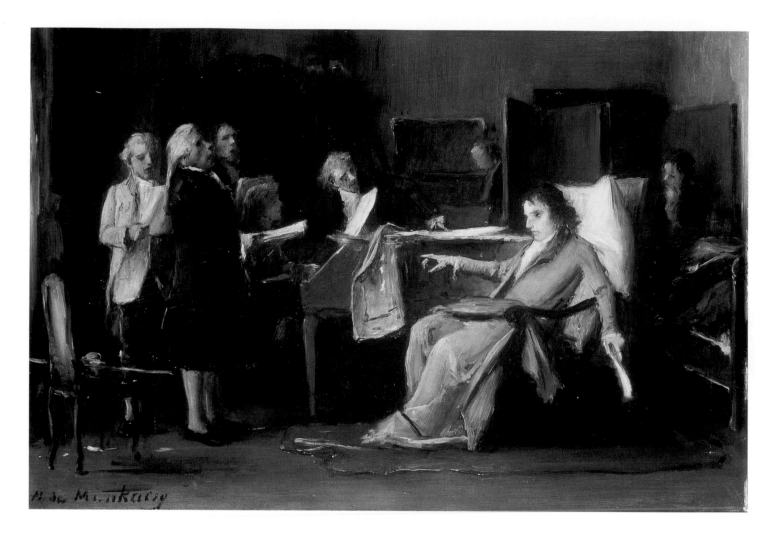

Throughout the summer, as he laboured on *The Magic Flute* and *La Clemenza di Tito*, Wolfgang Amadeus felt increasingly unwell. Doctors tried in vain to diagnose the illness. We now believe he suffered from uremia, a kidney disease. It was certainly made worse by lack of rest.

On 30 September he was only just well enough to conduct the first performance of *The Magic Flute*. The show was an instant success. Sadly, though, the composer's life was drawing to a close. He died at 12.55 a.m. on 5 December 1791, aged thirty-five. The Requiem, commissioned by a local nobleman for his young wife, remained unfinished.

An artist's impression of the last hours of Wolfgang Amadeus, listening to a first sing-through of his Requiem.

Constanze was overcome with grief and climbed into bed beside her dead husband. Later she recovered sufficiently to accompany the corpse to St Mark's Cemetery. Here, witnessed by only a handful of mourners, the body of one of the world's greatest musical geniuses was hastily laid in an unmarked grave.

'Stay with me tonight; you must see me die. I have long had the taste of death on my tongue, I smell death ...' Mozart speaking to his wife Constanze as he lay dying.

The manuscript of Wolfgang's last, most tragic work – the Requiem.

His Talent Lives On

Constanze recovered from her husband's early death and remarried. For the rest of her life she lived off Wolfgang Amadeus' reputation, which she strove to enrich. Even so, the exact place of his grave was forgotten. Not until 1859 was a marble monument raised in the vicinity.

W. A.
MOZART

1756-1791

'It may be said that untold tears were shed for Mozart; not only in Vienna, perhaps still more in Prague, where he was loved and admired. Every connoisseur and lover of music considered his loss irreplaceable ...'
Franz Xaver Niemetschek speaking about his friend Mozart in 1808.

The monument that marks the approximate resting place of perhaps the most gifted musician the world has ever known.

The Mozarts' surviving children did not inherit their father's talent. Karl Thomas, a minor official in Milan, died in 1858. Franz Xaver was an able musician but could not live up to his famous name. He died in 1844.

During the nineteenth century a new 'romantic' style of music came into fashion. Even so, the formal (or 'classical') music of Wolfgang Amadeus Mozart remained very popular.

In the later twentieth century, with both classical and romantic styles seen in a longer perspective, Wolfgang Amadeus' reputation soared. By the time of the bicentenary of his death in 1991, it was widely accepted that we will probably never see such genius again.

The performance goes on: a modern production of Wolfgang Amadeus' The Magic Flute.

45

Glossary

Anonymous Without a name, by someone unknown.

Chamber music Music for a small group of instruments.

Clavier Early form of piano.

Commission Pay for a new work of art, such as a piece of music, to be created.

Compose To write music.

Concerto A piece of music played by an orchestra and a solo instrument, such as a piano or clarinet.

Coronation Ceremony in which a crown is placed on a ruler's head.

Count Nobleman.

Countess Wife of a count.

Empire A group of lands governed by one country.

Harpsichord Keyboard instrument in which the strings are plucked.

Libretto The words of a song or opera.

Mass A service in the Roman Catholic Church.

Opera A serious play in which the words are sung rather than spoken.

Orchestra Many instruments that play together under the leadership of a conductor.

Prodigy Someone who shows unusual talent at a very young age.

Requiem A religious service for the soul of someone who has died.

Seraglio A building where Muslim rulers kept their many wives.

Smallpox A deadly disease that often left survivors with ugly scars.

Symphony A large piece of music for an orchestra.

Further Information

Books

Mozart and Classical Music by Manuela Cappon, Francesco Salvi & Hans Tid (Barron's Educational Series, 1998)

Young Mozart by Rachel Isadora (Viking, 1997)

Mozart by Wendy Lynch (Heinemann, 2000)

Lifetimes: the Story of Wolfgang Amadeus Mozart by Stewart Ross (Belitha, 2002)

Mozart, Young Music Genius by Francene Sabin & Yoshi Miyake (Troll Communications, 1990)

Wolfgang Amadeus Mozart by Mike Venezia (Children's Press, 1995)

Introducing Mozart by Roland Vernon (Chelsea House, 2000)

Date Chart

1756, 27 January Wolfgang Amadeus Mozart born in Salzburg, Austria.

1760 Begins music lessons with his father, Leopold Mozart.

1761 Composes his first music.

1762 First public performances in Munich and Vienna.

1763–66 Leopold Mozart takes his genius son on a tour round many countries, including the Netherlands, France, England and many German states.

1764 Writes his first symphony.

1767 Writes his first piano concerto.

1769–71 First visit to Italy.

1772 Hieronymus Colloredo becomes prince-archbishop of Salzburg.

1777 Leaves for Paris. Falls in love with Aloysia Weber.

1778 Mother dies in Paris.

1779 Court organist in Salzburg.

1781 Resigns from position in Colloredo's court. Living in Vienna. Meets Joseph Haydn. Writing the opera *The Escape from the Seraglio*.

1782 Marries Aloysia Weber's sister, Constanze. Writing a series of fine piano concertos.

1784 Karl Thomas Mozart born. Joins Freemasons.

1785 Begins work with da Ponte on the opera *The Marriage of Figaro*. Finishes series of Haydn string quartets.

1787 Meets Beethoven, a promising young composer. Prague commissions *Don Giovanni*. Leopold Mozart dies. Made minor court composer for Joseph II. Writes *Eine kleine Nachtmusik*.

1788 Writes his last symphony, no. 41 (later called the 'Jupiter').

1789 Visits Berlin. Revolution breaks out in France. Heavily in debt.

1790 Frequently ill. Attends coronation of Leopold II in Frankfurt.

1791 Franz Xaver Wolfgang Mozart born. Writes his last piano concerto, his clarinet concerto, *The Magic Flute* (opera) and his unfinished Requiem.

5 December, dies in Vienna, aged 35.

Museums and Festivals

There are several Mozart museums in Salzburg, Austria, the town of his birth. Information can be obtained from

Internationalen Stiftung Mozarteum Salzburg,
Schwarzstraße 26
A-5020 Salzburg, Austria

There is also a Mozart museum in Prague, the Czech Republic.

Each year festivals of Mozart's music are held not just in Austria but all over the world.

Index

All numbers in **bold** refer to pictures as well as text.